ScienceWork

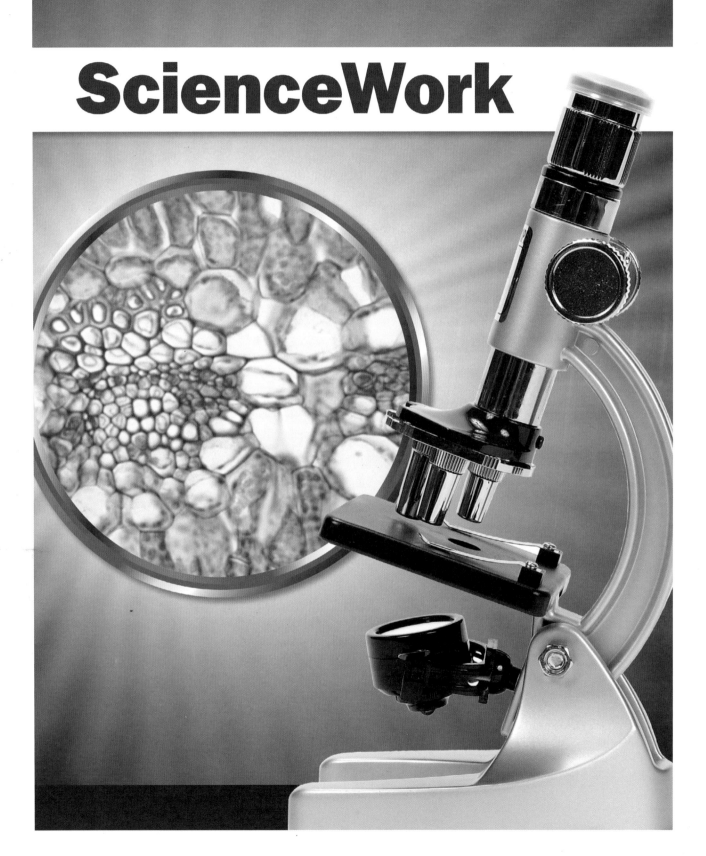

ScienceWork

**By Ginevra Courtade, Bree Jimenez,
Katherine Trela, and Diane Browder**

Editing by Linda Schreiber
Graphic design by Elizabeth Ragsdale
Illustrations by Beverly Sanders and Gabe Eltaeb

An Attainment Company Publication
ISBN: 1-57861-664-6

**Attainment
Company**

**P.O. Box 930160
Verona, Wisconsin 53593-0160 USA
1-800-327-4269
www.AttainmentCompany.com**

Contents

Unit C: Waters

Unit D: Chemistry

Appendixes

Unit  Earth

The cool crust

1 The first layer of Earth is the core. It is

in the center of the Earth. The core is made of hot,

solid metals and some hot, liquid metals. The second

layer is the mantle. It is made of hot, thick liquid

rock covered with cooler, solid rock. The third layer is

the crust. It is made of cooler, solid rock. We live

on the Earth's crust. We cannot live on the mantle

or the core. The mantle and the core are too hot

 for people to live on.

What we learned in class

The   Earth   has   different   layers.

Directions: (Circle) the best answer.

1   There   is   a   movie   named   **Journey   to   the   Center   of**

the   Earth.   What   layer   is   the   center   of   the   Earth?

the crust	the mantle	the core

2   What   is   the   first   layer   of   Earth?

the mantle	the crust	the core

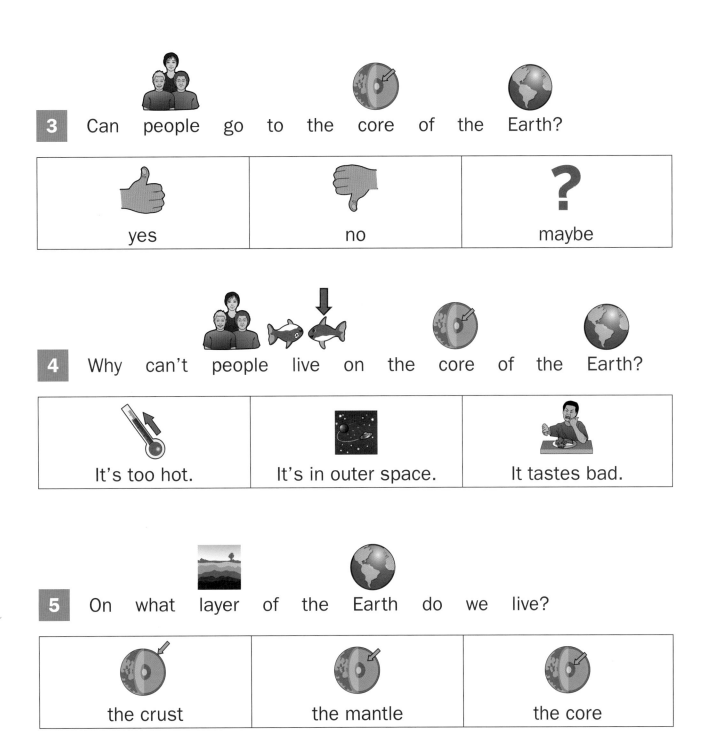

3 Can people go to the core of the Earth?

yes	no	maybe

4 Why can't people live on the core of the Earth?

It's too hot.	It's in outer space.	It tastes bad.

5 On what layer of the Earth do we live?

the crust	the mantle	the core

A bone from the past

  Fossils form in a certain kind of rock. It is

  called sedimentary rock. Sedimentary rock starts out as

      sand and mud. Animal bones are pressed into the sand

     or mud. After many years, the sand and mud harden

    and become rock. An imprint of the animal bones can

   be seen in the rocks. Another kind of rock is called

     igneous rock. Igneous rock starts out in the hot, liquid

layer of the mantle of the Earth. The  hot liquid

 melts the animal bones before they can make an

 imprint in igneous rock.

What we learned in class

Fossils   are   imprints   that   tell   about   the   past.

Directions: (Circle) the best answer.

1 A   fossil   is   an   imprint   of

an igneous rock	a living thing from long ago	a book

2 Fossils   form   in

sedimentary rock	igneous rock	a pillow

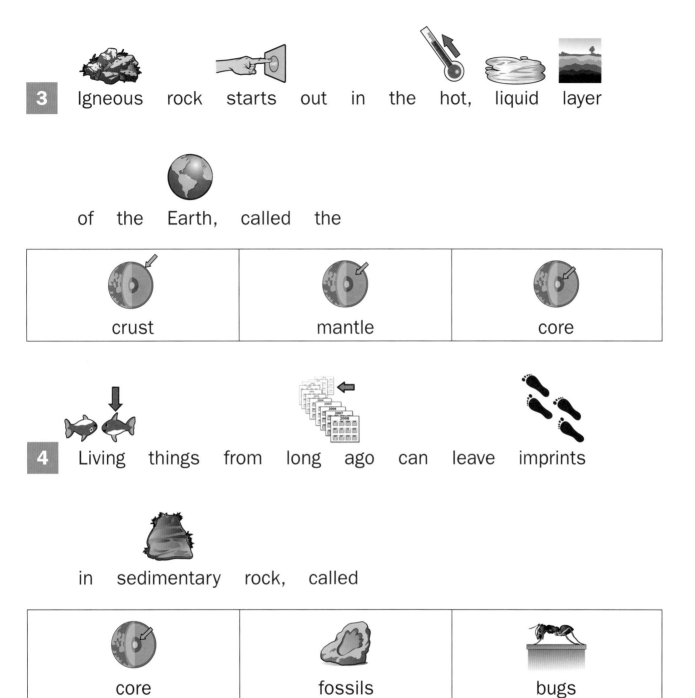

3 Igneous rock starts out in the hot, liquid layer of the Earth, called the

crust	mantle	core

4 Living things from long ago can leave imprints in sedimentary rock, called

core	fossils	bugs

Pushy plates

 Mountains form when plates bang into each

other and force the edges of the plates to push up.

When earthquakes happen, the Earth's crust breaks apart

as the edges scrape past each other. Sometimes the

movement pushes the Earth's mantle up, causing

a volcano to erupt. Volcanoes can be seen where

the Earth's plates come together.

What we learned in class

Plate movements cause changes

to the Earth's crust.

Directions: (Circle) the best answer.

1 Many years ago, the edges  of two plates banged

into each other. The edges of the plates were

  pushed up. What formed?

mountains	rivers	a volcano

2 In San Francisco, the edges   of two   plates

  pulled away from each other. What happened?

a snowstorm	an earthquake	a lightning strike

3 In some places in Hawaii,  plates   push against each

other and force   the hot   inner layer of the Earth

  to come out onto the crust. What happens?

Rivers dry up.	Lakes are made.	A volcano erupts.

Layers tell time

 Rocks that formed long ago are covered up

 by new rocks. Then another new layer covers up the

2 second layer of rock. Scientists found animal shells in

 old layers of rock. Then they found animal bones in

 new layers of rock. This told scientists that the first 1

 animals on Earth probably had shells. Animals with bones

 lived after animals with shells.

What we learned in class

Earth's   layers   tell   us   the   age   of   a   fossil.

Directions: (Circle) the best answer.

1   Rocks   that   have   imprints   are   called

fossils	core	Earth

2   Sedimentary   rocks   are

in outer space	made in layers	in the ocean

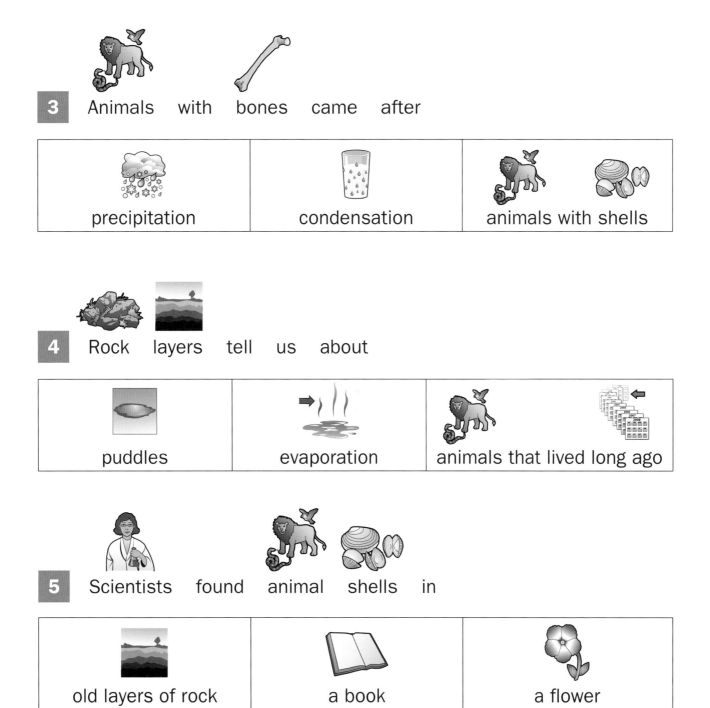

3 Animals with bones came after

precipitation	condensation	animals with shells

4 Rock layers tell us about

puddles	evaporation	animals that lived long ago

5 Scientists found animal shells in

old layers of rock	a book	a flower

Reuse means recycle

Some city parks have benches made out of

 recycled plastic. The plastic comes from plastic bottles.

Some winter jackets are made from recycled plastic.

The plastic comes from soda bottles. Some playgrounds

have swings made from recycled plastic. The plastic

comes from plastic shopping bags. Instead of throwing

plastic in the trash, it can be reused.

What we learned in class

Many materials can be used again.

Recycle means to use again.

Directions: (Circle) the correct answers.

1 Plastic shopping bags can be recycled to make

jackets	swings	sheets	benches

2 These things are made of plastic:

milk bottle	tree	pop bottle	shopping bag

3 We can recycle

dogs	newspaper	plastic	aluminum

4 Soda cans are made out of

bones	aluminum	paper	plastic

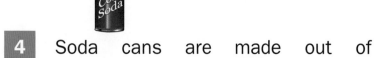

5 The best thing to do with paper is to

burn it	recycle it	eat it	spray it

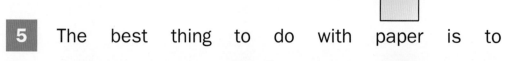

Unit B Biology

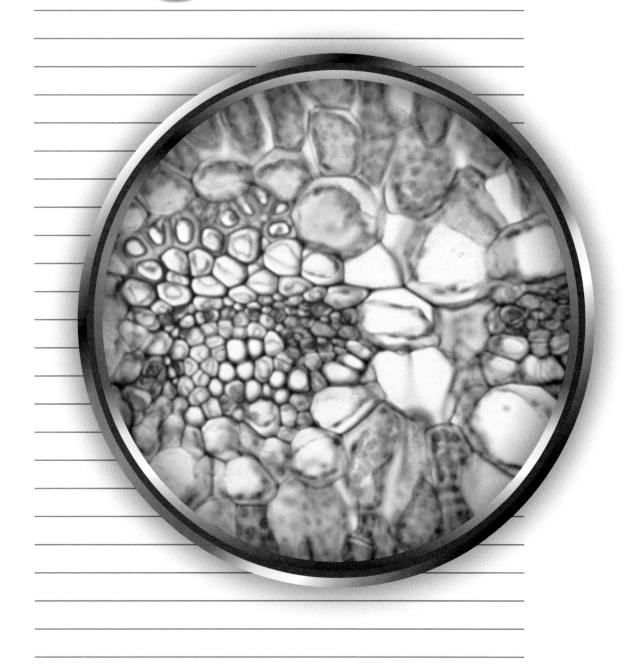

Cells mean life

 Animals have special cells that help them move.

 Animals also have cells that help them  see, hear, touch,

 and smell things. Plants have cells that turn the sun's

 light into green leaves. Plants also have cells that take

 in water and food from the soil to grow.

 Rocks are not alive. They do not have cells.

They do not move, eat, or grow. Rocks are formed

from materials in the   Earth's layers. Fossils are imprints

 of living things from long ago. Fossils are not living.

  Fossils are rocks.

What we learned in class

Living things have cells.

Directions: (Circle) the best answer.

1 I help arms and legs move. I am

an animal cell	a plant cell	a rock

2 I take in water and food from the soil. I am

an animal cell	a rock	a plant cell

3 I make green leaves from the sun's light. I am

a rock	a plant cell	an animal cell

4 I am an imprint from a dinosaur. I am

an animal cell	a fossil	a plant cell

5 I help eyes, ears, hands, and noses do their

jobs. I am

a rock	a plant cell	an animal cell

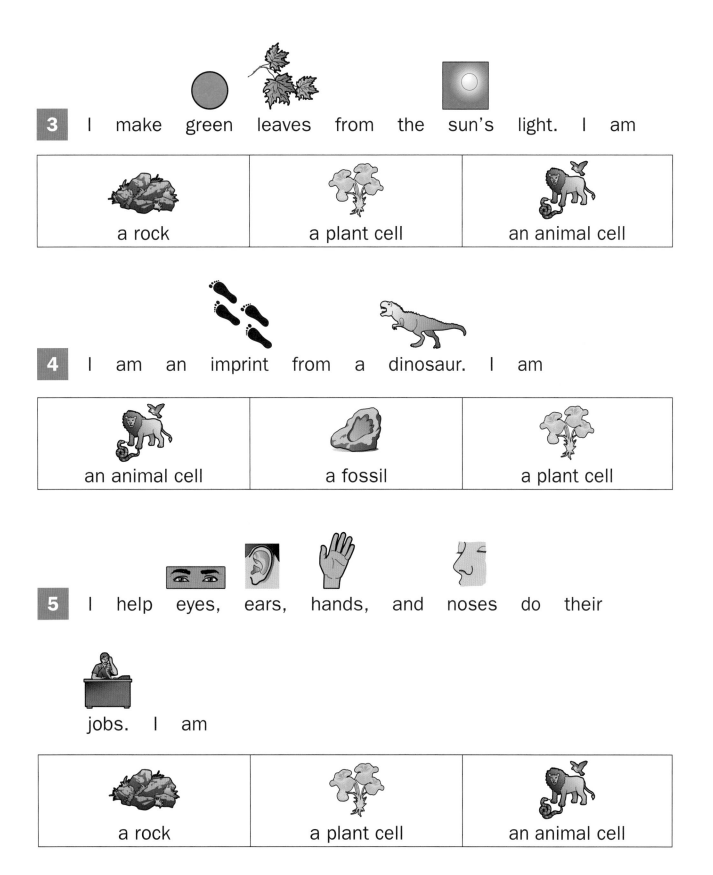

3

Three   main   parts   found   in   all   cells   are

the   nucleus,   the   cytoplasm,   and   the   cell   membrane.

The   nucleus   is   the   control   center   of   the   cell.

It   controls   movement,   growth,   and   taking   in   food.

Under   a   microscope,   the   nucleus   looks   like   a

dark   spot   in   the   middle   of   the   cell.

The  cytoplasm is a solution of many small

molecules  of food dissolved in liquid. Molecules of sugar

and protein in the cytoplasm help keep the cell working.

The cell membrane is like a big plastic bag.

That bag holds all of the cell parts   and fluids inside

the cell. It also keeps nasty things outside of the cell.

What we learned in class

Cells   have   parts.

Directions: (Circle) the best answer.

1   Which   cell   part   is   a   solution?

the cell membrane	the cytoplasm	the nucleus

2   Which   cell   part   is   the   control   center   of   the   cell?

the cell membrane	the nucleus	the cytoplasm

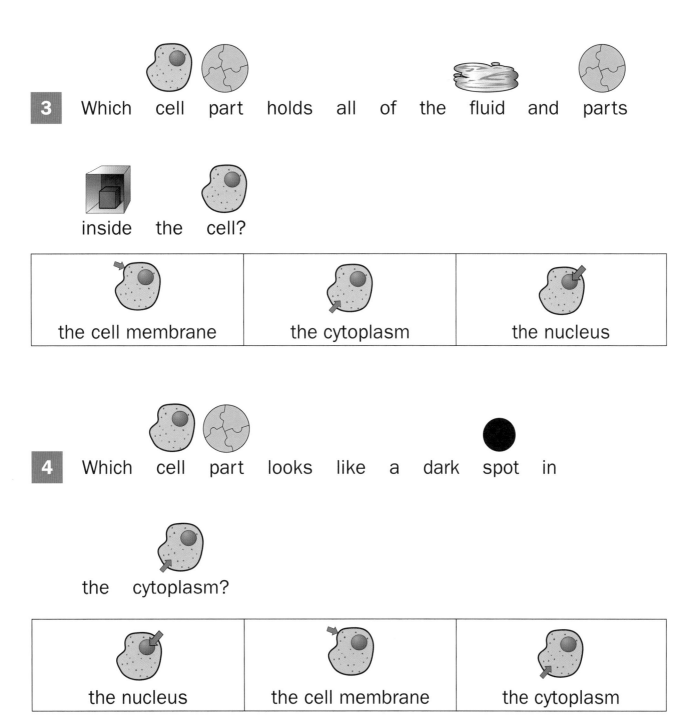

3 Which cell part holds all of the fluid and parts inside the cell?

the cell membrane	the cytoplasm	the nucleus

4 Which cell part looks like a dark spot in the cytoplasm?

the nucleus	the cell membrane	the cytoplasm

Divide and grow

1

One way that cells help living things grow is

by splitting apart to make a whole new cell. The name

for this kind of cell division is mitosis [MY TOE SIS].

 **1**

In mitosis, all of the parts that were in the first cell

are also in the new cell. Cell division makes all living

things grow.

What we learned in class

Cell   division   makes   living   things   grow.

Directions: (Circle) the best answer.

1   What   do   cells   do   for   living   things?

make them grow	make them sleep	make them eat

2   How   do   cells   help   living   things   grow?

They listen.	They eat.	They divide.

2 A scientist looked at a cell with a microscope. She

 saw that all of its parts stayed the same. It did

 not divide. What can you say about the cell?

It's growing.	 It's not growing.	It's a disease.

3 How do you know your cells are dividing?

You sing.	You sleep.	You grow.

Antibiotics and bacteria fight

Sometimes we have too many bacteria cells

growing in our body. Bacteria make us feel sick.

If we go to the doctor, the doctor might give us

medicine called an antibiotic. An antibiotic will break

down the bacteria's cell wall. Then our cells that fight

against disease rush into the bacteria cells and destroy

them! When the antibiotics begin to destroy the bacteria,

we   start   to   feel   better.   But   we   must   finish   taking   all

of   the   antibiotic   medicine   to   make   sure   that   the   bacteria

will   not   start   growing   again.   This   is   why   the   doctor

tells   us   to   finish   all   of   our   medicine,   even   when   we

are   feeling   better.

What we learned in class

Soap   destroys   bacteria   that   can   cause   disease.

Directions: (Circle) the best answer.

1   To   destroy   bacteria,   wash   with

medicine	soap	fruit

2   To   destroy   bacteria   in   your   body,   use

soap	antibiotics	water

3  Bacteria made Jenna sick. Her doctor prescribed

 an antibiotic. Jenna feels better after five days,

 but she still has five pills left. Can she stop

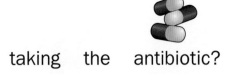 taking the antibiotic?

yes	no	ask a scientist

4  Stop taking an antibiotic when

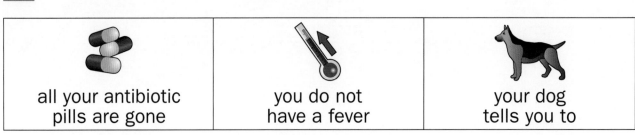		
all your antibiotic pills are gone	you do not have a fever	your dog tells you to

Good nutrition = healthy cells

  Different foods have nutrients to keep our

 bodies healthy. Bread foods have carbohydrates that

 help our cells store energy. Vegetables and fruits have

 vitamins to keep our skin and disease-fighting   cells

  healthy. Milk foods have calcium to keep our bone

 cells healthy. Meat has protein to keep our  muscle  cells

healthy. When we eat a small amount of each

 of these foods, we help all of the cells in our

 body stay healthy.

What we learned in class

Good   nutrition   helps   build   healthy   cells.

Directions: (Circle) the best answer.

1   Milk   foods   have   calcium   for   our

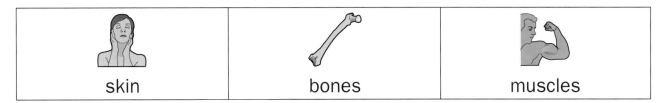

| skin | bones | muscles |

2   Meat   foods   have   protein   for   our

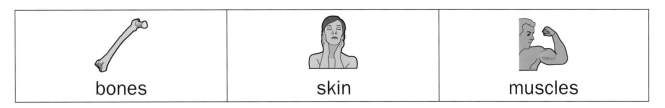

| bones | skin | muscles |

3 Fruits   and   vegetables   have   vitamins   that   help   our

bones	skin	muscles
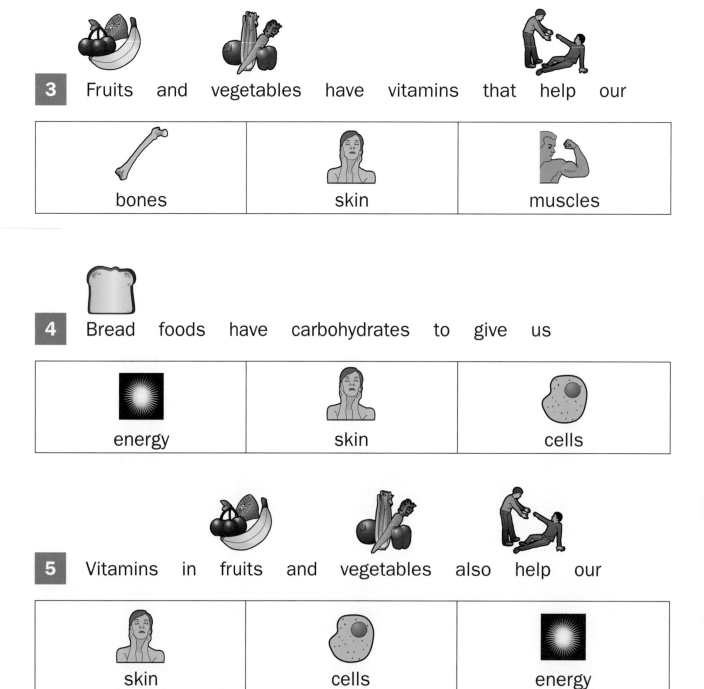

4 Bread   foods   have   carbohydrates   to   give   us

energy	skin	cells

5 Vitamins   in   fruits   and   vegetables   also   help   our

skin	cells	energy

Unit  Waters

The different forms of precipitation

When water droplets in a cloud get heavy, they

fall out as precipitation. The temperature of the air near

the ground makes different forms of precipitation. Two **2**

forms of precipitation are rain and snow.

The air high above the Earth is very cold.

When a cloud is full of water droplets, the water may

be ice crystals or snowflakes, even on a hot summer

day! In summer, snowflakes fall out of the clouds

way above the Earth. If the air temperature near the

ground is above freezing, the snowflakes melt and the

precipitation is rain.

In winter, snowflakes fall out of the clouds too.

If the air temperature near the ground is below freezing,

the snowflakes don't melt. Then the precipitation is snow.

What we learned in class

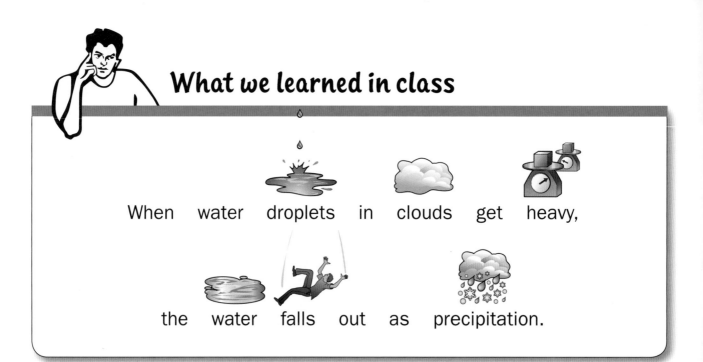

When water droplets in clouds get heavy, the water falls out as precipitation.

Directions: Draw lines from each air temperature to the form of precipitation that will hit the ground. Tip: **32°F = freezing**

Air temperature	Form of precipitation
10°F	
	snow
90°F	
20°F	
0°F	
	rain
60°F	

Water evaporates

When the heat from the sun warms the water

on Earth, the water turns into steam. Another name for

steam is water vapor. Water vapor is always in the air.

This is because of evaporation. Most of the water that

evaporates from Earth comes from the ocean. Water from

wet ground, rivers, and lakes also evaporates.

What we learned in class

When water is heated, it turns

into steam. This is called evaporation.

Directions: (Circle) the best answer.

1 What heats the oceans, lakes, and rivers on Earth?

a stove	a refrigerator	the sun

2 What is another word for water vapor?

steam	candy	dirt

3 Where does the water vapor go when ocean

 water evaporates?

into a cup	into the air	into a stove

4 What goes into the air when water from oceans,

  lakes, rivers, and puddles   evaporates?

water vapor	birds	candy

Steam is condensation

When water vapor goes into the air, it rises

high above the ground. Water vapor is the science word

for steam. The air high above the ground is very cold.

When water vapor is cooled by cold air, it turns into

water. The droplets of water collect to form clouds. This

is how condensation takes place in our world.

What we learned in class

When steam is cooled, it turns

into water. This is called condensation.

Directions: (Circle) the best answer.

1 When water vapor goes high into the air, it is

heated	happy	cooled

2 When water vapor is cooled, it becomes

condensation	evaporation	precipitation

3 Condensation happens when water vapor is cooled

 and turns into

the sun	a refrigerator	water

4   When the clouds are heavy with water droplets, the

   water falls to Earth. This is called

evaporation	precipitation	condensation

Keeping our waters clean

    1

Everyone can help keep our water clean. One

way is to keep leftover cans of paint out of the

trash. Paint has chemicals in it. When trash goes to

the dump, it's put into the ground. The chemicals come

out of the paint can and go into the ground. The

water that runs through the ground takes the chemicals

into rivers and streams, then into oceans. Special places

in our communities, called hazardous waste sites, will get

rid of leftover cans of paint for us. Some students

collect old paint cans. Then they have an adult take all

of the paint cans to the hazardous waste site. Having

  1

a special collection day for old paint cans is one way

to help keep our water clean.

What we learned in class

 Putting something in our water that

  harms living things is pollution.

Directions: (Circle) the best answer.

1 What does paint have in it?

food	chemicals	trash

2 Where does trash go when it's taken to the dump?

in the ground	in the clouds	in a lamp

3 How can chemicals get into the ground?

from a bed	from steam	from paint

4 Where do the chemicals in the ground go?

to school	to rivers	to lunch

5 What do chemicals in paint cause?

condensation	precipitation	pollution

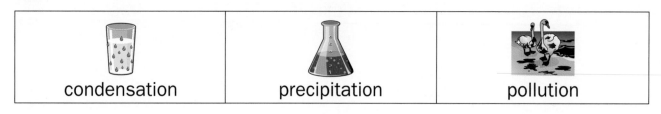

Saving water for the future

There are many ways people can use less

 water in their homes. One way is to take shorter

 showers. A second way is to use the dishwasher only

when it's full of dishes.  A third way is to fix leaky

 faucets. These are some of the ways that people can

 use less water in their homes.

What we learned in class

 Conservation means using less water.

Directions: (Circle) the best answer.

1 If we follow the rules of water conservation,

we take

longer showers	shorter showers	a nap

2 Water conservation means you

save water	save mountains	save pizza

3   If we follow the rules of water conservation,

   we wash dishes when the dishwasher

 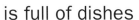		
is full of dishes	has a few dishes	is hungry

4 If we follow the rules of water conservation,

 we fix faucets when

they're working OK	they're dripping water	they're sunny

Unit D Chemistry

Solutions in nature

There are solutions in nature that help plants

live. The soil has food, called minerals, in it. Rain

mixes with minerals in the soil to make a solution.

A plant's roots take up the solution. This solution

helps the plants build strong roots and stems, and

grow leaves and flowers.  The solutions in nature help

plants live and grow.

What we learned in class

Solute + solvent = solution.

Directions: (Circle) the best answer.

1 What is the solute in the story **Solutions in Nature?**

the minerals in soil	the plant stem	rain

2 What can you find in the soil?

minerals	soap	rainbows

3 What is the solvent in the story?

minerals in the soil	the plant stem	rain

4 How does the solution get into a plant?

a straw takes it up	plant's roots take it up	animals step on plant

5 What does nature's solution do for plants?

helps them grow	destroys them	makes them sick

Chemical reactions in your body

 Your body is made of chemicals. The food

 you eat is made of chemicals. Your body needs the

 chemicals in food to live. When you eat, the chemicals

 in your mouth, stomach, and intestines mix with the

 chemicals in the food. The chemicals have a reaction to

 make new chemical mixtures. Your body uses the new

 chemical mixture to live. This process is called digestion.

What we learned in class

Some mixtures have a chemical reaction.

Directions: (Circle) the best answer.

1 When you eat food, chemicals in your _____

mix with chemicals in food.

shoes	stomach	chair

2 Digestion happens in your

stomach	eyes	face

3 The mixture of chemicals in your stomach and

chemicals in the food make a

chemical reaction	tree	mouth

4 Your body needs chemicals in food to

sleep	sing	live

5 Your body is made of

broccoli	feathers	chemicals

Garden solutions

Some chemical solutions kill bugs in gardens.

The solutions are called pesticides. Gardeners spray

pesticides on the fruits and vegetables to keep the

bugs from eating them. But pesticides can make us

sick. A better way to keep bugs from eating the fruits

and vegetables is to grow plants next to them that

bugs don't like. The bugs will stay away. This is called

organic gardening. With organic gardening, our food

won't have chemicals on it that make us sick.

What we learned in class

Solutions   can   cause   different   chemical   reactions.

Directions: (Circle) the best answer.

1   In   the   story   **Garden   Solutions,**   the

solutions   are

bugs	pesticides	food

2   Some   gardeners   spray   pesticides   on   their

desserts	candy	plants

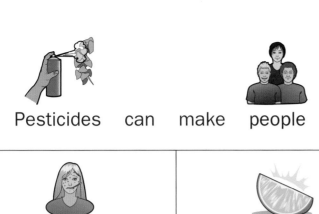

3 Pesticides can make people

sick	fresh	happy

4 Instead of using pesticides, you can keep

bugs away with a

plant	banana	bug

5 Organic gardening means you don't use

bananas	dogs	pesticides

A sweet solution

A special drink served in the South  is

  sweet tea.   Sweet tea is made with tea, sugar,

and boiling water. The sugar dissolves faster in the

 boiling water than in cold water. Boiling water can take

 more sugar than cold water. More sugar makes the tea

 taste very sweet. This is why sweet tea is made with

the special solution of boiling water and sugar.

What we learned in class

Solutes   dissolve   faster   in   hot   solvents

than   in   cold   solvents.

Directions: the best answer.

1   In   the   story   **A   Sweet   Solution,**   the   solute

is   the

 boiling water	 sugar	 fruit

2 The solvent is the

| boiling water | sugar | fruit |

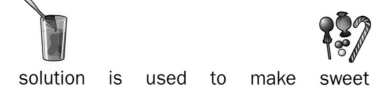

3 The solution is used to make sweet

| soda | tea | ice cream |

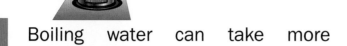

4 Boiling water can take more

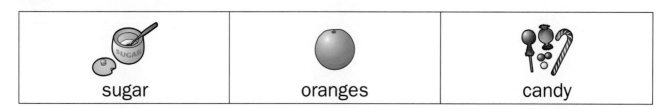

| sugar | oranges | candy |

The best solution

 The best solution for cleaning windows has a

 mild acid in it to take away oil and dirt on the

 windows. The best solution for cleaning wood has a

 small amount of oil in it to keep dust off the wood.

 The acid solution is helpful to the windows but is

 harmful to the wood. The oil solution is helpful to

 the wood but is harmful to the windows.

What we learned in class

Some   chemical   solutions   are   harmful.

Some   chemical   solutions   are   helpful.

Directions: (Circle) the best answer.

1   Acid   solution   is   _____   for   cleaning   windows.

helpful	harmful	cold

2   Acid   solution   can   take   away   oil   and

oranges	dirt	temperature

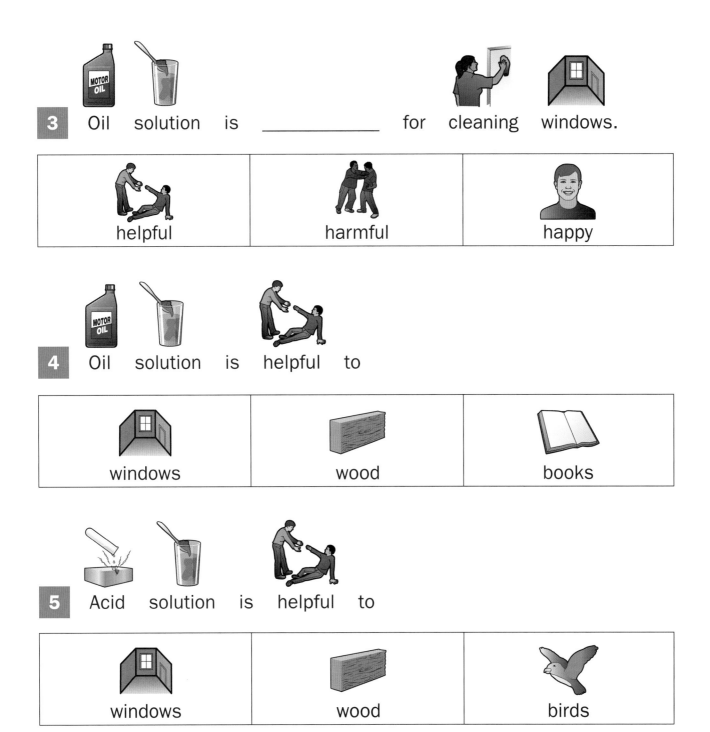

3 Oil solution is _____ for cleaning windows.

helpful	harmful	happy

4 Oil solution is helpful to

windows	wood	books

5 Acid solution is helpful to

windows	wood	birds

Appendixes

Using models in science

In science, sometimes we learn about things

that we cannot see or touch. Many times the objects

scientists study are too small to see. Other times,

the objects scientists study are too big and cannot be

touched. Sometimes the object is too old. When we

need to study something too small, too big, or too old

to see or touch, we use a model.

Have you ever seen a model car? It's very

small, not like a real car. We can still learn about

cars with our model. We can look at the parts and

how they are put together. We pretend that the model

is a real car.

Sometimes we need to pretend in science.

For example, a real house would be hard to make,

but we could make a model house with blocks.

Models are very important to scientists. Models

help them learn new things. Models can help us learn

new things too.

Earth's layers recording chart

Circle what was found in each layer of the model of Earth.

In Layer 3 we found:		Date formed _____	
fish	arrowhead	bone	nothing

In Layer 2 we found:		Date formed _____	
fish	arrowhead	bone	nothing

In Layer 1 we found:		Date formed _____	
fish	arrowhead	bone	nothing

Sorting labels

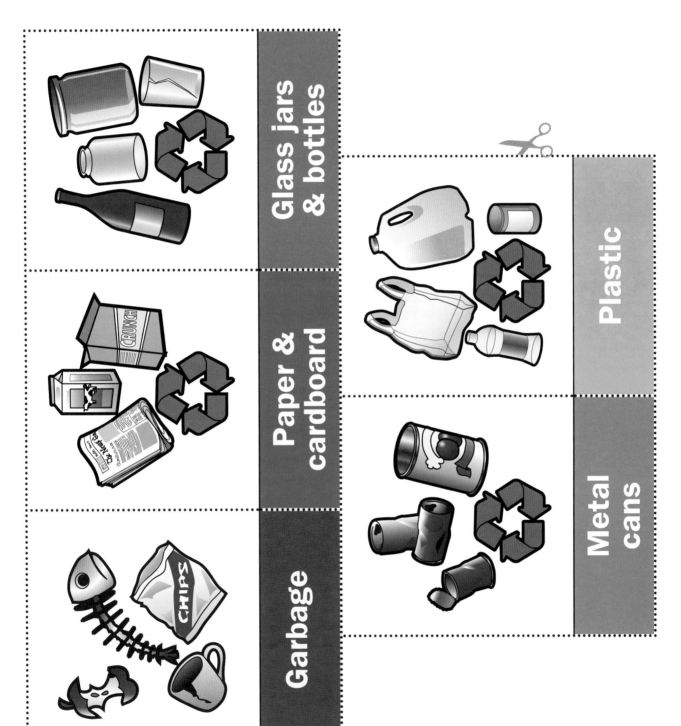

Glass jars & bottles

Paper & cardboard

Garbage

Plastic

Metal cans

Nutrition chart

Vitamin or mineral	How it helps the body	Foods containing the vitamin or mineral
Vitamin E	Helps form and protect body tissue & aids in the maintenance of red blood cells	
Vitamin A	Good for vision & healthy skin cells	
Vitamin K	Helps blood to clot so bleeding stops	
Vitamin D	Helps build strong bones & teeth	
Folic acid	Helps the digestive system	
Vitamin B6	Helps develop the nervous system & blood cells	
Vitamin C	Helps build strong bones & teeth	

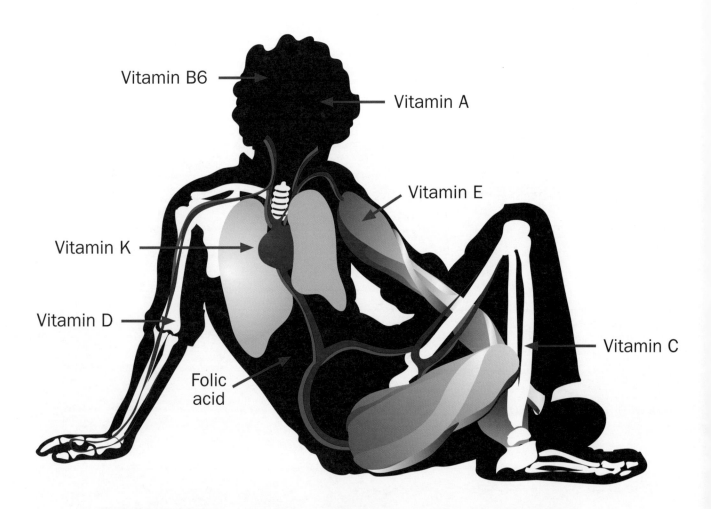

How vitamins and minerals keep us healthy

My food pyramid

GRAINS   VEGETABLES   FRUITS   MILK   MEAT & BEANS

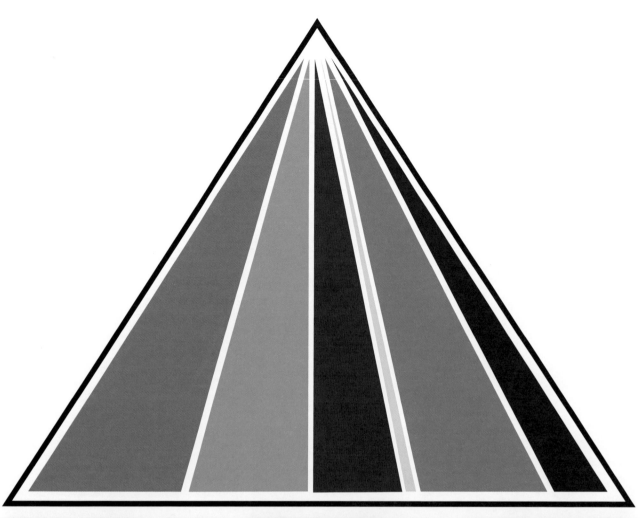

GRAINS	VEGETABLES	FRUITS	MILK	MEAT & BEANS

GRAINS	VEGETABLES	FRUITS	MILK	MEAT & BEANS

Grains

Vegetables

Fruits

Milk

Meat & beans

Earth's water is important to us

We use water every day. Water is very

important to living things. We use it many times

a day. We use water when we wash our cars.

We use water when we wash our clothes. We also

drink water and use it to bathe, to cook, and to

clean the house.

Water is in our streams, oceans, rivers, and

 lakes. That water comes from precipitation. It is pumped

from the ground to your house. You get water when

you turn on the faucets in your house.

 Without water we could not survive. We need

 water to live. It is important to learn about the water

on Earth and keep it clean and safe.

Do your part to conserve water

Take shorter showers.

Turn off water while you brush.

Turn on dishwasher only when full.

Fix leaky faucets.

What is a chemical reaction?

You will know you've seen a chemical reaction if:

1   The mixture bubbled.

2   The mixture changed color to one you didn't

expect. For instance, if you put red Kool-Aid® into

water, you would expect it to turn red. But if it

turned green, that would be a chemical reaction.

3 The mixture became hot or cold.

4 The mixture (if liquids) became solid.

Observation of the plants

Date your observation. Circle what you saw.

Date	Plant 1	Plant 2